The Simplified Personal Budget Book

I0414111

The Simplified Personal Budget Book

Personal Finance

Dewayne Gleeton

ISBN : 1-59457-807-9

To order additional copies, please contact us.
BookSurge, LLC
www.booksurge.com
1-866-308-6235
orders@booksurge.com

The Simplified Personal Budget Book

Contents

'Oh that Thou would bless me indeed, and enlarge my coast [territory], and that Thine hand might be with me, and that Thou would keep me from evil, that it may not grieve me!'
1 Chronicle 4:10

Note to the reader

Welcome reader, if your company or organization has purchased this book for you, it is an indication of how much of a value you are to your organization. This is a great time to become financially savvy and more informed about your personal financial situation. People have trouble managing their money for many reasons. This book, with its simple but fundamental instructions can help you become a better financial manager of your money. This book has been designed to be used with my workbook under the same name. I have included a coupon for half off the workbook price for everyone that has purchased this book. I hope and pray that each of the readers of this book find peace of mind in their finances. I must also inform you that this book is for educational purposes only and you should consult a professional financial advisor for specific advise about your situation.

Acknowledgments

I must first thank my wife Patryce for all of her support and confidence in my always-crazy ideas. I want to thank my children Brandee and Kelsee for their contributions to this book and for the joy that they bring to my life everyday. I want to also thank my father, James Gleeton and my uncle, Eugene Gleeton, for their wisdom and love. What would I be without that old Mississippi wisdom taught to me by these to great men? Also a special thanks goes out to my church family and pastor at First Baptist Church Broad avenue for the spiritual support and atmosphere for growth that I really need.

Introduction

Personal financial issues have always been one of the major problems of people living in these United States. Also, as an African American, these types of problems can and usually are even more amplified because of the societal pressures and restrictions that are in place. Personal finance is one of the most important aspects of life that must be mastered, if true happiness and fulfillment is to be accomplished. In this century and beyond, the level of debt allowed by people will be historically recorded as the new type of slavery applied to keep everyone in their societal place. However, this vital set of skills, personal money management, is not taught in our schools and usually, poorly taught in our homes. As members of this great society, we want more than anything, to have the best of things in life, and also we want stability and peace of mind. Without good personal financial skills and knowledge, these things, cannot be achieved with the longevity that we desire. In this book, you will learn all the basic skills needed to manage your personal finances and achieve your financial goals. Each area will be discussed in simplified terms and language. I will provide examples and analogies that are easy to understand and apply to your life. It is of course up to you to apply the knowledge and skills presented in this book to your life. Any abilities, skills and knowledge without consistent application aren't worth much. This is a working book, with information included that can be used throughout the year to manage your budget, and set financial goals. Also, I will introduce my "modular method"

of budgeting. This is what I feel is an excellent way to manage your income and expenses; giving you the control you need to accomplish your financial goals. Lets get started.

Dewayne Gleeton

I Dedicate This Book To My Father And Uncle. They Are Truly My Heroes In Life.

Laying in the grass
Feeling the sun on my face
The blue color flooding the sky
I feel the first day of summer

Green leaves on tall trees
With birds shouting their calls
Bicycle rides, pool parties, and long car trips
Sleepovers bring old friends back together

Independence day fireworks
Light up the July sky
Barbecue scents fill the air
Playing with friends until the streetlights come on

Back to school sales at the stores
While we savor the very last bits
Remembering that we could do it all again
But we will have to wait
Remember summer

Brandee Gleeton

Budgeting

In our financial lives, there are seasons. As we get out of high school and began our adult lives, we are starting anew, getting credit, and earning money. This is the springtime. Then we began to enjoy our things, the new car, the jewelry, and other possessions that we obtain. This is our summer. When the debt begins to mount and the creditors start to call for their payment, we know that this is a change in the weather for the worst, the fall. Finally, we are at a point where we need help. We can no longer finance our wants, and our financial future looks bleak. And we know that we are in the winter. Many times when I am in the winter months, I wish for that warm balmy day with bright sunshine and fun. Sometimes, I wish that it would be that way always. Financially, don't you wish you were always in that good space, where you were not over run with debt, and had enough money for what you needed, some of your wants, and you had peace of mind? A budget can help you reach that point. Winter is almost over, and the spring is waiting to start anew, Start your budget and stick to it.

Business Model

When you need to buy some gum or get a soda, you may sometimes stop at the Stop and Shop store on the nearest corner. This store is part of the cornerstone of the American economy. Of the trillions of dollars earned by businesses in this country a majority of the money is earned by the small businesses just like this Stop and Shop. All businesses large and small must operate effectively to survive. The key to each one surviving and thriving is a strong and adequate financial management system. Accounting systems for business are the cornerstone of this financial management system. Just like a small business your household should utilize a system for tracking your funds and financial situation. From this point forward, **you should consider your household a small business**. Lets call it "Your Name Inc." Like any business your main financial goal will be to maintain a yearly profit, and control your expenses. Also, your business, "Your Name Inc," will want to build assets and provide adequate protection for its employees, and property. *Your first step toward financial stability and strength is a budget*. How can someone like a famous singer, or boxer, earn millions of dollars and then end up in bankruptcy? They did not utilize a personal budget. What is the purpose of a budget? The purpose of a budget is to help your savings grow, to help you in getting all that you need and some of your desires. Most importantly, it is designed to enable you to reach your most cherished *future* desires. What is the first step in the budgeting process? **The first step is to get a snapshot of your present financial picture**. Without knowing exactly where you are, how can you know where to go? This financial snapshot is called a balance sheet. A balance sheet is used by businesses to assess their financial strengths and weaknesses and you should utilize one to do the same thing. Get out a blank sheet of paper. On the left side list everything you own. This includes your home, car, jewelry, electronics and savings. In the right column make a list of all the things that you owe money on. This includes cars, credit cards, doctor bills and loans. Also include your taxes owed on your property and income. Now subtract what you owe from what you own, and put that remaining number on your sheet in the bottom right corner. You have just created a balance sheet for your small business. This is a snapshot of your present financial picture. Is your net worth, the number that you placed in the right hand corner of your worksheet negative? Is it less than you thought it would be? This is the first step toward identifying where your money is going. Your balance sheet information can be used in many different ways. To help you get a loan from a bank, or to manage your cash. However, the most important purpose for having a balance sheet is to see how all of your uses of your income are interrelated. There are three important parts to a balance sheet. These are the assets, liabilities and net worth. Your assets and total liabilities and net-worth should always be the same. This is because your net worth is equal to your assets minus your liabilities. One important aspect to consider and recognize is the type and duration of your liabilities. How much long-term and bad debt do you carry? Long-term debt usually is any debt over two years in duration. This includes loans, auto payments and mortgages. Believe it or not, your credit card debt should be a short-term debt, because theoretically, it can be paid in full when the monthly statement is received. When should you complete a balance sheet? Some companies complete a balance once a year, while others do it semi-annually. I feel that it is best to initially complete a balance sheet either monthly or quarterly.

Income statement

This will help you to see your progress as you plan and manage your finances. Using our modular technology budgeting system will help you complete this task simply and efficiently this available in our workbook designed to be used with this book. The next important tool that you should use in management of your budget is the income statement. I described your balance sheet as a snapshot of your financial situation, a picture of your present financial situation. The income statement is more fluid. Your income statement will show you your actual financial actions and decisions as they occur during the period from when you start the statement to when it ends. It is just like watching a soap opera. Lets say the income statement starts at eleven and ends at noon; you will be able to see everything that happens in between. If you do a monthly income statement, you will be able to see what happened from the first to the thirtieth. If IBM did not track its expenses and income streams, how long do you think it would last? Not long. The only entities that can spend more than they earn and survive for an extended period of time are government entities. In order to manage your personal finances, you have to know where all of your resources are going. Furthermore, you must ensure that you do not have more going out than you have coming in. **Management of your cash flow is the number one problem in balancing and controlling your budget**. Could some one have an annual income of fifty thousand dollars and annual debt expenses of forty thousand dollars and be in financial trouble? The answer is yes. What about debt expenses of thirty thousand with the same income? Again the answer is yes. Both of these examples leaves a small amount of discretionary income, money not needed for bills, for the person to spend on a monthly basis. If this amount is wasted or exceeded, then all of the budget can be thrown off and this person will have severe financial difficulty. Here is an example. Mr. Jones has an annual income of $50,000. He will only have a monthly income of $4,166. The monthly expenses on annual expenses of $40, 000 would be about $3,333. This would leave only $832 for monthly discretionary expenses such as food, gas, entertainment, education and clothing. This is about $200 a week. The problem in this situation occurs when the Mr. Jones spends over $200 dollars on any given week for his discretionary expenses. Another way to look at this picture is to recognize just how much money is there for Mr. Jones to save and enjoy after the expenses and needs are met. He has a very high monthly income, with very little left over to reach the desires of his heart. On average about fifty dollars a week would be left savings and future goals. The income statement, unlike your balance sheet, will only show your sources of incomes and expenses. One thing that you must remember is that **your income is a limited resource**. This resource, because of its limitations, must be managed, and guarded and used in the most efficient way. You can only spend a dollar one time. In my financial planning practice, one of my favorite questions have clients ask themselves when making spending decisions was "*What better other thing can I do with this money.*" You see, there are many choices that can be made, and for each choice, there are two certainties that result. The first is that you cannot use that money again. Secondly, the choice you made will have a definite result or reaction. For example, if you decide to get a new car with a down payment of one thousand dollars, you have made a choice that cannot be changed. That money is spent. Furthermore, the future result or reaction to this choice will be the loss of a portion of your monthly income for several years.

Was there a better other thing that could have been done with this money? Definitely yes! For instance, the old car could have been used and the money that would have been a car note saved and invested for a number of years. Then the funds from this account could have been used to purchase a car with a down payment, and the monthly payments made from the same account. You have purchased a new car, but kept your extra cash flow from your income available for optional uses. By the way, this is called a "car fund". If you know that your income is a limited resource, and that you must operate like a business, then in order to ensure a profit, **you must manage your cost**. **The money earned as income, must be more than the money spent as expenses**. In your budget, you should try to follow several simple but steadfast rules. Firstly, you should control your expenses. When you first began to work, your level of income was far lower than it is now. However, you were to live off of it comfortably weren't you? If you sample a room of people, say in a movie theater, many of them will be at totally different income levels. Ranging from twenty to one hundred thousand dollars a year or more. But, most of them would say that they do not have enough money! All of these people are saddled with debt and a small amount of extra cash flow. These facts are true because unless we control our expenses, our expenses will always grow to equal our income, no matter how high it goes. Human nature is that our wants are unlimited. Unfortunately, our

Save Now

Incomes are limited. Secondly, you should also begin to save money for the future. Most of us under the pressure of debt assume that there is no way to start saving money. How can we if we cannot even pay all of the bills? The answer is that you can and you must begin now. My father always told me to save ten percent of what I make. He would always ask me, "Are you putting some money back?" **You must save money for your future and for those rainy days**. Get a glass and a water pitcher, now fill the glass ten times and each time pour the glass of water into the pitcher. Now pour one glass of water back into the glass. Look at how much you still have left in the pitcher. You have more than enough water in the pitcher to quench the thirst of many people. In this way, when you save ten cents of each dollar you earn, you will find you can still do what you need to do as far as bills and other expenses. The benefits of beginning to save are a sense of financial achievement and the knowledge that you have something that is yours. *Start now to save ten percent of what you earn*. The third rule that you should apply is to increase you income streams. I have spoken about the fact that our income is a limited resource. Also, in the African American community, it is viewed in a negative light to do more than one job. I worked for sixteen years at Local Corporation. At this company, when I began to start my own business or get other sources of income, the other black employees would talk about it in a very negative way. "You must be Jamaican," they would say in very negative tones. What they did not realize, and what I was just beginning to understand, was that by learning new skills, and owning a business, or getting another job, no matter how small, expanded my options, and raised the wall of my limitations a little higher. How many businesses succeed and prosper with only one product and one source of income? How risky would this be? What is the stability level of a building's roof with only one pillar holding it up? **Increase your income and knowledge**. Give your small business a more stable and less limited income level by more than one stream of income. Don't let the other crabs pull you back into the bucket.

Future value of every dollar spent

When you spend a dollar, what does it really mean? Firstly, as I explained before, you cannot use that dollar anymore. Your money is just like time. Once it is used, it is gone. Furthermore, by deciding for that specific use of the dollar, you have also chosen against all other possible uses for it. Let me repeat this important fact again. *When you choose to spend your money on one choice, you are also making a decision against all other possible uses, some of which could be infinitely wiser*. Another very important consideration that you are not making, and this is one I often stress with my clients to make when formulating their financial plan, is that each dollar is more valuable than you think. In business, *there are many considerations of the future value of choices and decisions made*. What is the future value of possibly your most important asset, your current income dollars? If you had an extra thousand dollars, say when your taxes came back with a refund, you would have to make a choice about what to do with it. Those choices could be, buy a new riding lawn mower, or use it for a down payment on a new car, or save it in a mutual fund. Each of these choices has a future monetary value. By getting the mower, you have spent the money, with no additional cash flow expenses to look at. Also the money is gone and cannot work for you. If you chose to get the new car, the money would be gone, and an additional cash flow expense would be created in the form of a car note. Thirdly, by putting the money in the mutual fund, you have put the money to work for you, with a possible future value of ten to twenty times what it started out as.

One Percent Strategy

How can you start to lower your expenses so that you can save ten percent of what you earn? A very good way to do this is by developing a one percent strategy. A one percent strategy is very simple but it is also a very powerful tool for giving you extra cash. There is a point in a company's business cycle when competition is very strong and there is little flexibility in pricing. Also, there are very few opportunities for this business to lower its costs of making the product it sells. When a business faces this type of situation, it must still develop ways to increase its profits. Many businesses will utilize a strategy of cost analysis in all of its areas of operation to cut costs. Each dollar cut from costs goes directly to the bottom line in the form of profits. The one percent strategy does the same thing for your small business. This is how it works, pull out your income statement and review each expense listed. Figure out one percent of each expense listed. Some of your expenses cannot be reduced, but many of them can and should be reduced by one percent or more. If you spend thirty dollars a week on lunch, and saved 5 percent on this expense, it would only add up to about $1.50 per week or $6 dollars a month. This is only a small part of our budget and is very easy to do. You will find that these small increments of 1 to 5 percent are easy to do. However, the sum is greater that the parts. Once you total up your full savings on a monthly basis, you will be surprised to see a huge amount of money that can be pulled from the expense column with little change in the way you live. Another way to look at this is to increase quality and efficiency of your business operations. Get three different color pens and make a copy of your income statement. Your first pen will be for cost analysis, use it to take one or more percent from all the expenses you can. Now use another pen to go through all of your expenses with the idea of quality analysis. Do you really need this expense in your life? Does it help the quality of it? Cigarettes could an example of an expensive habit that gets cut by the quality of life pen. Now use the third pen and go through the statement with the idea of efficiency, what are my waste categories? Where are the places in my budgets where I can be more financially efficient? The choice of which grocery store used can often mean the difference of fifty to one hundred dollars a month in expenses in the food category. Once you have utilized the one percent strategy and the three-pen-method you will have seen several ways to decrease your expenses and increase your monthly cash flow.

Borrowing and how to make it work

❧

Borrowing money can be the downfall of any successful business. When a business carries too much debt, it can too often result of the business going bankrupt. However, all of the most successful businesses borrow money in a way that works positively for them. As you manage your small business, Your Name Inc, you must utilize the same strategies that are used in the business world to *make your borrowing work for you*. When you make borrowing decisions, it is important to make them with the end result in mind. Too many times we make consumer debt borrowing decisions. We borrow money for cars, jewelry, bills, and even clothing. The only time that most Americans borrow money for positive investments are home purchases and college tuition. By the way, college tuition borrowing is only good in this sense if the student completes college. I suggest that you consider borrowing money for investments purposes. Invest in bonds, stocks, real estate, and any other investment vehicle that you are knowledgeable about and feel comfortable using. Once my Uncle, Eugene was clearing a field to plant some cotton. He had farm in Mississippi where he grew cotton, corn, peas and cows. In the middle of this field was a large tree stump. I as a young boy was spending the summer down there and I was in the field to help out with the chores. The thought I had in my mind was how my cousins, my uncle and me move this huge stump. My uncle Eugene said, boys move back over there under that shade tree, and let me get to work. He was going to move it by him self? Of course me and the other boys moved over to the tree and watched. My uncle pulled out a small jack looking thing that was attached to a chain and some pulleys. He attached this chain to the stump and then started cranking the jack. With each turn the chain moved, became tight and in no time, the stump was coming out of the ground. After my uncle had finished removing the stump, he came over and talked to us boys. He said, "Now what I used to remove that stump was the leverage generated by that pulley system to tremendously increase my strength. Boys, remember to be smart and use leverage to increase what you can do on your own." Believe it or not, you can use leverage for more than moving large tree stumps. Leverage in the investment world is using borrowed money to increase the amount of money to put into an investment. Most people have heard of the big shot stockbroker buying stock in his margin account. This is the use of leverage in investment purchases. However, you do not have to be a stockbroker to use this powerful technique. It is important that you consider that the investment that you borrow money for is one that will increase in value. What are some of the benefits of using leverage? Firstly, leverage can help you get involved in an investment sooner than you could have with only your own money. For example, I wanted to invest in a company called Back Yard Burgers. At the time, the stock was selling for less than two dollars. I really did not have the money I wanted to make the investment. So I did not do it. If I had used leverage and borrowed say $10,000 dollars, to make the investment, I would have been able to sell it in 2004 for about 8 dollars a share. This is a four-fold increase from the initial purchase price. Secondly, leverage can increase the profit your own investment dollars make. For example, if I had put $5,000 of my money with $5,000 borrowed money; the investment described above would have grown in value from $10,000 to $40,000; with the leveraged earning half of this investment increase. The important thing to remember is that leveraging works best only when the profit from the investment will be greater that the cost of the loan. You would not borrow money at 12% interest to invest in a vehicle that would only earn 3% interest. There are many ways to borrow money to invest. These include bank loans, credit card advances, finance companies, and margin accounts. I feel that the best vehicles to use for borrowing for investment purposes are the second mortgage, 401k /403b retirement plan, or life insurance. These three vehicles have unique benefits that suit them best for this or any type of borrowing needs. Firstly each of these vehicles usually has low interest rates for their loans. The second mortgage loan rate is currently at a historically low point. Many banks and companies want you to get this loan to pay down credit card bills, or pay for extravagant vacations. But, would it not be better to use it in a smart investment. Also, the interest payments on a second mortgage loan are usually tax deductible. Coupled with a low rate, this makes the cost for this loan very low. Investment of funds from these loans into moderately conservative investments that earn 6% or more can go a long way in increasing your assets and future financial strength. For example, say you have a first mortgage with twenty years left on it and $30,000 in equity in the home. You get a second mortgage on the home for $25,000 at 5% for twenty years. This will give you a monthly payment of $164.99. Also, the interest payments on the loan would add up to $14,597, if the loan were paid for the whole twenty years. What are the benefits? $25,000 invested for twenty years with an 8% annual return would equal about $123,000. Plus, you would get tax deductibility for most of the twenty years further reducing the cost of the loan. Not only can you manage your finances in the same ways as a small business. You can also act as your own bank! How great would it be if you could apply for a loan, guarantee that you would get it, and then when the loan is paid back, the principal and interest goes right back to you. You would feel like a banker wouldn't you? Getting money out of a 401k/403b or a variable life insurance policy can give you most of these benefits. Your retirement plan should have provisions for you to borrow money from your account and how to pay it back with interest. The great thing about this is that your payment plus interest goes directly back to your account balance. For example, you borrow $20,000 dollars as discussed above from your account to make an investment. The loan payment of $164.99 would be divided up into two payments of $83, if you were paid twice monthly, or about $42, if you are paid weekly. As long as the loan is paid back within the terms, there should be no tax consequences, and the payment and interest goes to directly to your account. There is no credit check, and you can have the payments payroll deducted. There are several more benefits to this type of loan. For example, the loans rate us usually very close to the prime rate. What's the best way to compare this loan to borrowing from somewhere else? The first thing that most people do is to compare the interest charged on the loan. The plan administrator sets the rate. The law says that it has to be a 'reasonable' rate. Let's say that the rate is 3% less than the rate that the mortgage company would charge. It is still a competitive rate, which goes back to you. Also you must consider what type of growth will be lost in your retirement plan if you take some of the money out. You will need to know how much to estimate your money will earn in the 401k plan if not borrowed. This is not an easy or precise estimate to get. The earnings will depend on how the money is invested and your average rate of return. Each retirement plan has different investment options. Some are very conservative and only offer conservative investments with a lower rate of return. Other plans are heavily invested in the stock of your company. Depending on the performance of that stock, your return can be terrific or terrible. Of course you should never put all of your eggs in one basket. The law specifies that the loan be repaid in less than five years or when the 401k is closed. One exception is that loans for a new home can be repaid over 30 years. This requirement can have important consequences. If you leave your job, you should expect to close your 401k. This is one consideration you should have before taking a loan from your 401k. If you do not pay the loan back when you leave your company, then you'll have to pay a 10% early withdrawal penalty and increase your income taxes by adding the loan amount to your income. The other vehicle you can use as your own personal banker is the cash value life insurance policy. This type of insurance policy should have loan provisions in the contract. Based on your available cash value amount, you can take a loan and use it for any reason you want. There are no governmental restrictions on what purpose you can use it for, or tax consequences involved as long as you don't surrender the policy. How does this work? Your life insurance starts out with a face amount value, this is the life insurance amount you purchased. Once you start to make payments, a part of the payments go toward the costs of the insurance and its administration, and the rest goes toward cash value growth. When you make a loan you have the option to pay it back or not. If you don't pay the loan back, it will usually take away from the face value of the policy when death occurs. However, There is away to make a loan, not pay it back, and keep your face value in tact. Many policies now have an option two choice for face value and growth of the cash value. This option two adds the cash value to the face amount value. As the cash value goes up, so does the face amount. So if you had a cash value of $20,000, after ten years of owning the policy. The face value would be the initial amount plus $20,000. This is a great way to get a loan and have very little pressure on your cash flow. Loans from your insurance can be paid back when you can afford to. There is no set payment plan or time frame. There are many advantages to this type of insurance.

Debt

Once I saw an odd drawing of a gold fish in its aquarium. What made it odd was that the aquarium was made out of a blender! A caption under the drawing said, " you think you got pressure!" If you are suffering from the totality of suffocating debt, then you know intimately what this picture is saying. Too much debt is one of the major causes of stress, unhappiness and depression. It is one of the major causes of divorce also. What is the definition of slavery? If you looked up the definition of slavery you would get something like this " Slavery is defined as a condition or subjection or submission, characterized by lack of freedom of action or of will. When you are overburdened with debt, you are in a slavery condition. You do not have any financial freedoms left, and the pressure and stress on your life continues to grow and affect your happiness. Why do we submit ourselves to financial slavery? Why would someone build a chain of debt and shackle it to him or herself? The reason that we do this is due to a lack of knowledge. Did you know that some consumer debt is designed to last thirty years or more? Many consumers are now financing cars with 72-month payment plans. Why would you finance a loan on an asset that at the end of the agreed upon terms, the asset would be worth 95 percent less than the loan amount? Again, a lack of knowledge is the cause for this totally inept decision-making. One of the most immediate and severe punishments for slaves in America was issued to the slave

that was caught trying to learn to read. The slave master

knew that as long as he kept the slave ignorant, he could keep him under his control. The slave master used this type of mental conditioning to control slaves that out number him a hundred to one. Just as not having education can keep you in bondage, the correct education, about what has you in bondage, can set you free.

Getting out of debt

How do you get out of debt? First and foremost, you must truly want to be out of debt. In the movie Roots, the slave Kunta Kente, wanted to be free so bad that he took off and ran through the night to escape slavery. When he was caught, he was viciously beat. A few months later, he tried to run for his freedom again. He kept on trying to escape and he kept getting beat. The only thing that stopped him from trying was when his foot was chopped off. Kunta Kente truly wanted to be free. However, there were slaves on the same plantation that never tried to be free. They became complacent in their life of slavery and did not ever want it bad enough to make a run for their freedom. For them slavery was not harsh enough to merit their trying to escape. *It is up to you to decide if your slavery, your debt situation, is harsh enough for you to make a change*. Do you really want to be free from the bondage of debt? Will you do what it takes to get there? If your answer is yes to these two questions, then you can be out of debt. I believe that the best way to get out of debt is also the simplest. Firstly, you must stop using credit. Total up your credit debt and make your first decision, and promise to yourself, no more credit. Believe it or not, you can live in this modern world without credit usage. I can say this for a fact, because I have done it for the past five years! Credit and the bad debt from it's over use should be listed as a major cause of death along with heart attack, car accidents, and smoking. Just as the a cigarette package is labeled with a warning, " cigarettes have been found to cause cancer and is hazardous to your health", credit cards should be labeled, " credit card usage has been found to lead to bad debt and enormous stress and is hazardous to your health and mental well being". What most American consumers don't understand is that for most of the things that they want and need, credit usage is not necessary. The annual median household income in the United States is $42,409 according to US census data from 2002. This equals $3,534 dollars a month. Without overwhelming debt, most of the things we need and want could be purchased out of our monthly budget. Let's imagine that we are not the typical American, that we are atypical, and did not start our adult life out with collecting debt. So all of the money we make is free for us to choose where to spend it. We would develop a spending plan and make purchases as needed. In the typical situation, we are cash flow poor; in the atypical one we are cash flow rich. In the typical situation, if we want a new HD TV that cost $4,500, we would finance it with a retail loan, with about 15% interest. With a payment plan of five years, your payment would be $107.05. In the atypical situation, it would be planned to save $1,125 for four months, and purchase the TV. By the time of purchase, it was found that the TV had dropped in price by $1,000 and only cost $3,500. The day after the TV is purchased, the cash flow amount returns to the original of $3,534. In this atypical situation, if a new washer or dryer is needed, they are paid for in cash. A new lawn mower; paid in cash. A new anything can be paid for with cash and the cash flow rich situation can be maintained. I realize that this is an ideal situation, in that debt was not created in the beginning. However, with perseverance and patience, you can pay down your debt and reach this cash flow rich situation also. As I stated, the way out of debt is with education. This education should begin with the acquisition of wisdom. **Wisdom is the key to you getting and maintaining financial peace**. Proverbs chapter 3 verse 13-17 says, " happy is the man who finds wisdom, and the man who gains understanding. For her proceeds are better than the profits of silver, and her gain than fine gold. She is more precious than rubies and all the things you may desire cannot compare with her. Length of days is in her right hand, in her left hand riches and honor. Her ways are ways of pleasantness, and all her paths are peace." With wisdom you have happiness, peace, riches, and long life. Further reading in the book of Proverbs points out the urgency and importance of getting wisdom. Proverbs chapter 4 verses 7-9. "Wisdom is the principle thing; therefore get wisdom. And in all your getting, get understanding. Exalt her, and she will promote you; she will bring you honor when you embrace her. She will place on your head an ornament of grace; a crown of glory she will deliver to you." Wisdom, education about your finances can and will bring happiness and peace to you and your family.

Six Cures

So you must first decide two things, I will stop making debt, and secondly, I will dedicate myself to increasing my financial education. Once you have made these two decisions, you can easily follow the following six steps. Earlier in this section, I described debt as an illness-causing agent. It can be looked at like a cancerous disease affecting your whole life. There are six medical treatments or steps that can be used to rid your life of this cancerous disease, debt. The first one is to **control your expenses**. Make it a part of your everyday habits to think about each and every purchase that you make. Decide to omit the ones that you truly do not need. Promise yourself that you will keep up with your expenses, and never again over spend past your allotted amount. For example, if your weekly budget for lunch is $25 dollars, $30 dollars for lunch, is now not acceptable. Use the methods in this book to cut your expenses and increase your cash flow. Controlling your expenses is the first step to getting out of debt. Over spending is analogous to smoking more and more packs of cigarettes each day. You will be making the debt stronger just as a smoker would make lung cancer more potent. The next step is to **start saving a portion of what you make for yourself**. When I was overwhelmed by debt, the last thing I thought I could do was save money. How could I save something, when I did not have enough to pay the people I owed? When someone first gets cancer, the last thing that they can think about is the future. They are looking at imminent death and cannot see themselves as a cancer survivor with a bright future. Something must be done in both situations to change the mindset that has occurred. When you start to save money, no matter how small the amount is, it will began to give you that positive outlook and a brighter future perspective. Look at it this way, before I began to save money in my 401k plan at work, I did not have enough money to pay all of my creditors. After I started saving I still didn't have enough money for them. Only time and perseverance would help me pay some of them off, and then free up money to pay the others. What changed was my situation after the debts were paid off. Without saving, I would have no bills, and no money saved up. With saving, I would be debt free, and have some money saved up for retirement. Along the way, the money I saved, was money I would have blown anyway on things like videos, food, other escapes from the pressures of life. I just had less money to blow! Does this sound like you at all? **Start saving now**. Many doctors say that the persons positive outlook, " I will survive this cancer" is just as important as the medicine in overcoming the disease. Saving will give you a positive outlook. The third step is to getting out of debt is to **increase your earning power**. I once heard an educational business tape by a guy named Jay Abraham. He is a well-known motivator and consultant to fortune 500 business owners and their top management. He was discussing the principle of exponential power. In his example he talked about how small increments in productivity over several different areas, would increase the productivity exponentially for the organization as a whole. If you increased the price of a product by 5 percent, and increased the sales, by 5%, and reduced the cost of producing the item by 5%, your overall profit would increase exponentially. You would result with a profit increase greater that 15%. Increasing your income while at the same time reducing your expenses will do the same type of thing for you. Would it be wonderful to get a part time job, or start a small business knowing the money earned is strictly for your investment or debt reduction goals? Getting an income increase and using it wisely to invest or pay down debt will speed up your financial plans. By the way,

paying down debt is an investment. If you have a credit card that has interest charges of 18%, by paying off the balance as soon as possible, you are saving 18% on those dollars. You are keeping money that you otherwise would have to spend. By having another source of income, you increase the strength of your family's budget. Remember, your business should have as many sources of income as possible. When someone has cancer, doctors often utilize an aggressive therapy program. This entails using several types of therapy to attack the cancer all at once. This increases the chances exponentially of totally eradicating the cancer. Fourthly, you should follow the basic debt reduction plan. By using this plan, you should be totally debt free within seven years. This statement includes mortgages and car payments. This plan entails paying off your debt in a set stage or sequence. This is how it works. First list you debts in order of balance owed. List from smallest to largest. You will focus your attention on the smallest debt first. Apply as much money from your cash flow as possible, and the regular payment to this bill. For instance, you have your smallest bill listed at $500 dollars. With a monthly payment of $25 dollars and $75 dollars more added from your cash flow, you pay $ 100 dollars a month toward this bill. All of your other bills will be paid the minimum balances required at this time. You will pay this bill off in five months. Now the next bill on your list is a loan for $1200 dollars, with a minimum monthly payment of $80 dollars. You will now focus your attention on this bill. You will add the $100 per month from the first bill; to the $80 dollars a month you pay on the loan. Paying $180 dollars a month, you will pay this bill of in about seven months. After one year, you have paid off $1700 dollars worth of debt, and now are on your third bill on the list. Lets assume this is a student loan account worth $5000 dollars. Your payment on this loan is $220 dollars. When you combine the payments you will now have $400 dollars a month to apply to this bill. After a year and a half, this loan would be paid totally off, and you can then apply this $400 dollars to your next highest bill, the car note. Your principle still owed on your car loan is say $12,000 with a payment of $500 dollars per month. Adding your payments together will equal $900 per month. You can now pay your car off in only 13 months later. You have now paid off all of your debts except your mortgage in about three and a half years. Now lets assume that you owe $60,000 dollars on a thirty-year mortgage. With twenty-three years still left on the mortgage. You have completed three and a half years of debt reduction and have $900 dollars to apply to the principle on your mortgage payment of $650 per month. By doing this your mortgage would be paid off in about 40 months. Making you totally debt free in less than seven years. It can be done. Part of the services that my company, DG Services, offers is a detailed plan for anyone that wants to reduce their total debt in about seven years. Why seven years? I feel that this is a period of time set by God, for all of his people to be released from debt. Deuteronomy chapter 15 verse 1-2: "At the end of every seven years thou shalt make a release. And this is the manner of the release: every creditor that lendeth ought unto his neighbor shall release it; he shall not exact it of his neighbor or of his brother; because it is called the lord's release. Of course your creditor will not follow this bible passage, but through the lord's will, have I not given you a plan that can help you be released from debt?

As a financial planner, my goal is to help people do the following fifth step or treatment, **plan for retirement and provide protection for you family.** In life, there comes a time when we all must stop working for our income. When this time comes, where will the money we need to maintain our livelihood come from? If we die next week, where will the money to maintain our family's lifestyle come from? The problem with us planning for these two eventualities is that we are selfish individuals. We have only excuses and more excuses for our selfish ways, to not plan for and protect our future. Its pitiful and your pitiful if you are still using these excuses not to do what must be done. Common sense is thrown out the window in most American households. What about yours? Is there any semblance of common sense being used? Here is the problem; people are living over their annual incomes for material things, like cars, clothes and the like. If you are living paycheck to paycheck during your working years, and not saving anything, what are you going to live off during your retirement years? Social Security? It will either be gone by then, or the age to receive some money will be extended into the eighties. Will your company provide money for you? Many companies present now, will have long gone bankrupt by your retirement age. Also, if you are not putting money in the company plan, then what can they match you with? Most companies give employees a percentage match, but if you do not put anything in the plan, then you don't get the match. Will you family or kids take care of you? No! You have successfully taught them, through you actions over the years, to be as bad off financially as you were. They don't have the money to help you with doctor's bills and the other stuff you will have in old age. What they will do is just sign you over to a nursing home when the time comes, because they have to go to work, as they are living check to check and cannot miss one, or they will sink. Since none of the above will work, and you already know that they won't, living your life as if they will is kind of crazy; isn't it? You must plan for the future. If you don't, what kind of future will you have? There is a simplified way to save for the future that anyone can do if they have the desire and will to. The steps include first, deciding what kind of retirement life you want to have. Most people want the same type of lifestyle in retirement that they have before retirement. If you are living off $50,000 a year now, then you will actually need more than $50,000 a year in your retirement years to have the same style of life. If you don't have retirement savings and a pension, then you would have to live in retirement on about 25% of your current income, which would be $12,500. Ask yourself "do I have a plan for the future? Your answer to this question is yes. **By not making a plan, you have in effect chosen a plan like the one described above, where you will only get the assistance given by the government at that time**. Let me give you a story as an illustration. My uncle Eugene was driving home one evening after a long day in the field on his big old tractor. He was going pretty fast for a tractor, as he turned a bend in the road. In the middle of the road was a young deer. As my uncle described it, the deer had plenty of time to move, but he could not decide to go back the way he came, or to finish crossing the road. So my uncle summed it up this way, when the deer could not make a decision, the forces of life made one for it. In effect, that deer had three choices. Go forward, go backwards, or die. By not choosing one of the others, he, in effect, chose to die. Once you have decided on your retirement lifestyle, then you can plan to on how to provide for it. Based on the time before retirement, assumed inflation rate, and percent of current income you want, and your assumed rate of return, you can determine how much money you need to save now, to reach your goal. Your first and best option for planning for retirements is to start saving in your company sponsored retirement plan. This is usually a 401K or 403B plan. Your company 401K plans have several advantages for you and your family. Firstly, the amount of money you save, is taken out pre-tax. This means that you will pay a lower amount of money to the government. People always complain about taxes, and here is a chance to do something about it. Secondly, the money you save in the plan can grow tax deferred. This is a powerful advantage for you, when planning for retirement. Each dollar that you save plus the earnings and the company match will grow and compound. Over time this is a powerful tool for reaching your retirement goals. Your company plan also gives you several choices of retirement investment that can fit your risk profile. Your risk profile tells you based on how much risk you like to take, what type of investments to put your money in. One of the greatest advantages to the company plan is that it comes out of your check before you get it. Out of sight, out of mind. Before you know it you will have a large sum of money saved up in your plan. Another overlooked but great advantage is the company match. Some companies give a certain percentage toward your plan account, while others give a flat amount as long as you reach a certain level if savings. For example, one plan that I know about gives each employee five hundred dollars if the save one thousand dollars a year. This is a

fifty percent return for the employee's investment of $1000. If
the mutual fund that the employee has invested in earns 10%,
then the employee will earn another $150 over the year. In two
years the employee will have saved $2000 of his or her own
money, but the account value would be about $3300. You can't
beat this type of growth outside of the company plan with as
little risk. Above all, start saving in the company plan now. Also,
you should provide for the future of your family if you happen
to die prematurely. If you save a small sum of money on a
monthly basis, with a good investment return, you will have
enough money for retirement. Would it be better also to be able
to save a small amount on a monthly basis, and even if your
family needed it in one week after it was started, all of the
money you could have saved for thirty years would be paid to
your family in it's time of need? This is in essence what insurance
is. Once you start your monthly premium, the small savings a
month, then your family will be paid a face amount, in their
time of need. Why would you, in your very tight budget, living
on a check-to-check basis, ensure that your auto and home are
insured? You feel that they are valuable and in the case of loss
you want them either replaced or repaired. What about you
ability to earn an income? Believe it or not this is your most
valuable asset. How valuable is a $50,000 a year income? Look
at it this way. What amount of money would you have to save up
to pay out at least $50,000 dollars a year, indefinitely, with
increases to match inflation? The amount would be worth some
where between $500,000 and a million dollars. Your ability to
earn an income has a present value of about a million dollars.
Should you not insure it against damage like your home or car?
The insurance needed to do this is disability insurance and life
insurance. You need these as your fifth step. When someone
has a disease infection, one of the best fighters or cures for the
disease is to introduce a vaccine into their system. The vaccine,
a weakened version of the real disease, once in their system will
start the immune response. One of the bodies' most important
defense mechanisms against infection is the production by the
body of a class of proteins called antibodies. When the body is

infected, it recognizes the virus as being alien to the body. These foreign cells release antigens, which stimulate the production of antibodies designed specifically to fight these antigens. The antibodies or immunoglobulins produced during the immune response have the capacity to bind to the antigen, triggering a series of reactions that lead to the destruction of the foreign cell. The thing that helps, the antibody, multiplies on its on to fight and cure the infection. In the case of your cancerous finances, the money that you are beginning to save can work the same way. Once I started saving, it became something that I wanted to do more of. Why, because of the sense of accomplishment that it gave. When you save $100.00, and it earns say three percent interest in a bank account, then the value would be $103.00. Now think of each penny in the initial $100.00 as an antibody. Each penny earned .03 cents of profit. Better yet, they never stop earning. Each year your initial savings, and the money added to it from interest will keep earning more interest. This is your sixth cure for the disease of bad finances. As I said before, you should start saving right away, even if your finances are not well right now. You wouldn't wait until you were well and then take your medicine would you? Don't wait to save! Here is another point, think of your dollars as your employees. You should not give them away, but put them to work for you in a savings account or investment.

Savings

Lets talk a little more about savings. As I mentioned in the last section you should start to save right away. Also, I have mentioned in different sections, several investments to save in. One of the most important aspects of savings is choosing the right type of investment. If you ever thought about investing and talked to anyone in the financial advice professions, then you have probably heard of such investments mutual funds, stocks, annuities, REITS, and limited partnerships. But have you ever heard of the COW investment vehicle? This is one of the best types of investments and usually does better than many of the familiar ones you have heard of.

Assets (farmer analogy)

Let me begin. My uncle Eugene and aunt Bernice had six children. They lived on a farm in Mississippi about fifty miles from Memphis Tennessee. On this farm, they some chickens, fields' cotton and corn, gardens with peas and greens, and a few pigs and dogs. They drove around in an old Ford pickup truck and used car. Also, my uncle had a few Cows. Everybody in the family worked on the farm, when the cotton was ready all the kids, and my aunt and us cousins, had to help chop and pick cotton. I spent my summers down there on the farm and chopped my share of cotton. My father and his brothers and sisters all insisted that their children get their education. So when my uncle's kids grew up it was time for them to go to college. Each of his six kids went to a small private college in Mississippi and with a car of their own, and they never wanted for anything!! How did this happen? The COW investment is the answer. You see every cow walking around on my uncle's farm was really something else. Each of my uncle's cows was what is called a revenue-producing asset. My uncle had about 100 cows and a huge bull to keep them happy. Each cow was worth about 700 dollars each. Walking around my uncle's farm was a living investment fund of about $70,000! But the great part of this is that each and every spring, 30 to 50 percent of those cows had a calf worth around $400 dollars. That's an annual profit of 12 to 20 thousand dollars a year. The return on investment in COWS equals 28.5 percent annually! The important fact to remember is that like my uncle, you should invest your money in assets that produce revenue. These include real estate, higher education, bonds, and a small business of your own. When making considerations about saving money, I have said several times, that you should save at least 10 percent of your income. *This is the minimum savings level you should have.*

80/20 Law

Another you should take into consideration is the 80/20 law. It is a law of nature that shows itself every aspect of our life. Here are some of the familiar facts based on this law. 20% of the people possess 80% of the wealth in the country. 20% of the people at church provide 80% of the money. 20% of the people carry 80% of the workload at church. 20% of the sales people make 80% of the sales of an organization. The law is true in all aspects of life. Some people are comfortable in the 80% range and others in the 20% range. Humanly speaking, the difference between the 20% and the 80% is that the 20% plan, have discipline, and organize their lives. There is also a difference in beliefs between the 20% and the 80%. Firstly, the 80% desire safety and want no big demands made on them. They do not want responsibility and are content to be like everyone else. This group wants to just get along and do not set goals for their lives and do not take chances in life. Anyone in the 80% group can change and become a 20% person. They must begin to enjoy competition, set goals for their lives and like to win. They should make a plan for their lives and work their plan. Another aspect of the 80/20 law is in savings. **Ideally, you should live off 80 percent of your earnings, and save 20 percent**. It can be done if you are sincere about your desire to have financial peace in your life. By following the information and ideas in this book, you should be on your way to this ideal way of living in no time. 80 percent gives you enough money to enjoy the pleasures of life, and the 20 percent is adequate enough for you to pay yourself 10% and to pay the10% that you owe to god. Blessings and peace will be yours by following this guideline. I have learned the hard way, that without doing what is right, my financial peace of mind would not come. When you consider Gods blessings to you for doing what he has asked of you in tithing, don't just consider what is being given to you. You greatest financial blessings could be coming from God by what he is keeping away from you! Your car hasn't broken down in years. There is no great sickness or injury in your family. The fine or expenses that you were supposed to get, was waived. Another point to remember is, when you are a good steward over what you have, you will then be blessed with more. Read the following passages in your bible. They should help you with understanding Gods power, judgment, and goodness. Read Job chapter 36 and 37. Also, read Isaiah chapter 3, verse 14 thru 24, and Mark chapter 10 verse 17-31.

What to do next

Consider that what you have in this book is a beginning guide for getting out of debt and starting to save toward peace of mind in your life. There are many other areas and financial topics that move forward from this beginning. You must begin with your budget first. Now that you have finished reading this book, it is then time for you to start using the knowledge that you have gained. Make out you list of bills, complete you income statement and do all of the things in this book that seem to fit your situation. Action is the key. Use the information in the book and order the workbook. Also, increase you knowledge, by reading other great books on personal finance. Make it a habit of reading and using, one or two great financial books a year.

About the Author and His Book

Dewayne Gleeton is a writer, consultant, and educator from Memphis Tennessee. He has spent ten years in the financial services industry as a Financial Planner and Advisor for such reputable companies as American Express Financial Advisors and Waddell And Reed. He is a notable speaker on the topics of budgeting and financial planning across the country. The idea to write a book using simple but strait forward principles and language was formed many years ago. This book and its companion workbook are designed to be read and used by all types of organizations to help their employees, and members to have financial peace of mind.

Quick Order Form

Website: www.dgservices.50megs.com

Email: dgleeton2002@yahoo.com

Postal: make check payable to: DG Services. Complete the form below and mail to: *DG Services, 6548 Margaux Cove East Memphis Tennessee, 38141.* **Include your name address, phone number and email address with your order.**

Please send me the following books and information. I understand that I may return any of them for a full refund – for any reason, no questions asked. **Add $3.00 for shipping.**

Choose one of the titles below:
1. ***The Simplified Personal Budget Workbook ($13.95)***
2. *Introduction to mutual funds (free)*
3. *Handbook to credit protection laws ($1.95)*
4. *A roadmap to financial security ($1.95)*
5. *Building a better credit report ($1.95)*
6. *Credit Solutions Program book(39.95)*
7. *Mortgage Minder System (29.95)*
8. *Saving fitness, a guide to your financial future ($1.95)*

Appendix I – Internet sites to help you find definitions of investment terms.

http://www.investorwords.com/

http://www.investopedia.com/

http://www.invesco.com.au/web/webdict.nsf/pages/index

http://www.raymondjames.com/gloss.htm
http://www.edwardjones.com
http://www.globefund.com/centre/Glossary_IFIC.html
http://www.econofinance.com/investterms.htm